The Radha Poems

*I was the boy who picked you flowers
a long, long time ago.*

excerpt pg. 69

Also by Jeevan Bhagwat

The Weight of Dreams
(IN Publications, 2012)

Luminescence
(IN Publications, 2020).

The Radha Poems

THE RADHA POEMS
by

Jeevan Bhagwat

720 Sixth Street, Unit #5
New Westminster, BC
V3L 3C5   CANADA

The Radha Poems

Title: The Radha Poems
Author: Jeevan Bhagwat
Publisher: Silver Bow Publishing
Cover Art: "Dancing in the Ether" painting by Candice James
Cover Layout and Design: Candice James
Editing: Candice James

All rights reserved including the right to reproduce or translate this book or any portions thereof, in any form without the permission of the publisher. Except for the use of short passages for review purposes, no part of this book may be reproduced, in part or in whole, or transmitted in any form or by any means, either by means electronically or mechanically, including photocopying, recording, or any information or storage retrieval system without prior permission in writing from the publisher or a licence from the Canadian Copyright Collective Agency (Access Copyright).

www.silverbowpublishing.com
info@silverbowpublishing.com
ISBN: 978-1-77403-355-5- paperback
ISBN: 978-1-77403-356-2 electronic book
© Silver Bow Publishing 2025

Library and Archives Canada Cataloguing in Publication
Title: The Radha poems / by Jeevan Bhagwat.
Names: Bhagwat, Jeevan, author
Identifiers: Canadiana (print) 2025016745X | Canadiana (ebook) 20250167468 | ISBN 9781774033555 (softcover) | ISBN 9781774033562 (Kindle)
Subjects: LCGFT: Poetry.
Classification: LCC PS8603.H36 R34 2025 | DDC C811/.6—dc23

The Radha Poems

**For our beloved Radha
none as cherished as you**

The Radha Poems

The Radha Poems

Contents

I	13
II	14
III	15
IV	16
V	17
VI	18
VII	19
VIII	20
IX	21
X	23
XI	25
XII	26
XIII	27
XIV	28
XV	29
XVI	30
XVII	31
XVIII	32
XIX	33
XX	34
XXI	35
XXII	36
XXIII	37
XXIV	38
XXV	39
XXVI	40

The Radha Poems

XXVII	42
XXVIII	43
XXIX	44
XXX	45
XXXI	46
XXXII	47
XXXIII	48
XXXIV	49
XXXV	50
XXXVI	51
XXXVII	52
XXXVIII	53
XXXIX	54
XL	55
XLI	56
XLII	57
XLIII	58
XLIV	59
XLV	60
XLVI	61
XLVII	62
XLVIII	63
XLIX	64
L	65
LI	66
LII	67
LIII	68
LIV	69

The Radha Poems

LV	70
LVI	71
LVII	72
LVIII	73
LVIX	74
LX	75
LXI	77
LXII	78
LXIII	79
LXIV	80
LXV	81
LXVI	82
LXVII	83
LXVIII	84
GLOSSARY	87
AUTHOR PROFILE	89

The Radha Poems

The Radha Poems

RADHA

The Radha Poems

The Radha Poems

I

These are the poems
I never wanted to write,
the ones whose words
are washed with tears,
and blended with the blood
of you.

II

Mother,
I have grieved you
for so long now,
before your heart tired of its rhythm
and ceased to sing its song,
before your body shrivelled
like rice paper
in the wrinkled hands of Time.

I have grieved you
when fear took hold of my ear
and poured its dark predictions
into me.

Flesh of my flesh
blood of my blood,
long before your departure,
I tasted the pain
of this truth;

I have been grieving you
for years and years.

The Radha Poems

III

It was a day like any other,
nothing different or special
or out of the ordinary;

you were up early, as usual
hot cup of tea on the kitchen table
buttered toast, slice of cheese,
a sizzle of scrambled eggs
resounding through the house
with the scent of childhood memories.

Sunlight flamed your russet hair
as you smiled at me with all of Autumn
descending in your sleepy eyes,

and I thought nothing of it
nothing at all,
were it not for that moment
when you clutched your chest
and my life as I knew it
changed forever.

IV

Dark Saturday,
3 o'clock,
the saddest of hours.

You left
without saying goodbye,
your felled body
cold and motionless
upon the carpeted floor.

We encircled you
holding hands,
a rosary of hearts
entwined with grief,
and recited prayers
while your soul took flight
on its long journey
heading back home.

The Radha Poems

V

The Linden tree looked solemn
the day you died;
a stillness hung heavy
in the afternoon air
like a teardrop suspended
upon a cheek,
refusing to fall or dry.

September sky was shattered
into silvery shards of light.
West wind wailed a requiem
as you spread your wings
and took to flight
into the beautiful blue unknown.

VI

A strange song sounded that morning
announcing his dark presence
as he came, uninvited,
and barged his way into your heart.

Spirit bird cried from solemn Spruce
while he waited patiently
to take your life
and lead you away from here.

The sky's seams burst
with relentless rain,
each of us drowning
in a deluge of tears,
unable to speak;
unable to breathe
our love back into your lungs.

The Radha Poems

VII

I had a bird, but it flew away
into a September sky,
I had a bird that could not stay
and so, it winged goodbye.

I long to see and hear her sing
her lovely melody;
but gone is she who once did bring
such happiness to me.

VIII

Your favourite dress
still hangs in the closet,
longing to wear you again.

Your bedroom slippers
that followed you everywhere
await your footsteps in vain.

Not much has changed
since you went away,
your hairbrush, earrings,
even your pillows
are fixed within their place;
a museum of artifacts
left behind
where the only thing missing

is you.

IX

Funeral day,
and you in your midnight blue dress
replete with polka dots
white as stars.

Twameva mata cha pita twameva

We stood solemnly
next to the casket,
adorned with blossoms of
red roses; our hearts
vined together in grief.

Twameva bandhushcha sakha twameva

At the podium
a Hindu priest recited old prayers
to guide the atman
on its journey home,
sang bhajans in praise
of a Vedic trinity
with a voice as ancient as rhyme.

Twameva vidya dravinam twameva

I held your hand
as we walked to the hearse,
whispered words of comfort
between streaming tears,
said I love you
even as my heart was breaking
with every slow step we took.

Twameva sarvum mama deva deva

At the crematorium
we gathered together,
your sons entrusted
with the final act,
as I laid you down
for the last time,
kissed the face that loved me
all my life,
and cried goodbye
in the heat of the flames.

Om shanti shanti shanti.

The Radha Poems

X

Early morning,
October sky splintered
into shards of light.

We walk hand in hand
down a sunlit lane
to where the river's mouth
sings fluvial.

I tell you about the dandelions
and their yellow insurrection,
where the maples yet dance
like jewelled ghosts
defying the gravity of
Autumn's stare,

and we reminisce about old times,
the joys and sorrows
that we've both shared
from living such intertwined lives .

The Radha Poems

Beyond a bridge
that straddles the riverbank
we find a clearing
through the underbrush,
a pebbled sanctuary where the trees
keep quiet vigils to themselves,
and we wade into the water
    together,
the shallow rapids
reflecting sky,
till I cut my heart open,
bleed it of its tears,

and scatter you in clouds,
angel white.

The Radha Poems

XI

Coming back home
where everything remains 'in situ'.

Not much has changed
since you went away;
your pots and pans
still hang in the kitchen
next to the living room
now emptied of your presence.

In the upstairs bedroom,
the closet still jealously
guards your clothes,
while a hairbrush rests
on the dresser top,
dreaming of your auburn hair.

But an emptiness lives here now,
a hollowing of space
that can never be filled,
for your heart was the hearth
that warmed our family,
and you will always be *home*
to me.

The Radha Poems

XII

I count the hours without you,
the slow, sad hours
of little consequence
when the heart feels nothing at all.

My calendar is a clock of days,
each one, a bucket
collecting tears
that empty into
the reservoir of time.

XIII

Beautiful Bird,
I held you close
that Autumn day
when your life song
ceased to play.

The love you carried
for each of us
was a weight you gladly bore,
but your heart grew frail
in your twilight years
and could carry that weight no more.

You were light as feathers
in my trembling arms
the day you said goodbye,
I watched your brown eyes go to sleep
just as you braved the sky.

The Radha Poems

XIV

There is a wound in my heart
no thread could stitch,
no glue could seal,
or balm could ever heal.

I will carry it with me
all the days of my life,
through the happy days of sunlight
and the sad days of rain,
through the in-between days
of laughter and pain,

that I will always be reminded
of what I had gained,
and what I have lost
in you.

The Radha Poems

XV

Memory is a thread
that binds me to you,
weaves through the narrative
of our intertwined lives;

but in the slow, sad hours
of mourning,
grief is the only
chronicler of time
when our story unravels
to an unfinished tale,
inked with the blood
of my heart.

XVI

*I grieve for having lost
that which was she:*

shy smiles that warmed me
on the coldest of days,
soft hands that mended
my torn-up heart,
a voice as light
as angel wings.

*I grieve in gratitude
for what you gave to me:*

a love so great
it swallowed me within,
wise counsel over breakfast
of scrambled eggs and toast,
Sunday mornings and homemade bread,
words of comfort that you said.

In the hollow days of mourning
I grieve for you and she,
for all that was given
and taken away from me.

XVII

Help me,
for I cannot go on much longer
in this tattered and shattered state.

I have drunk deeply
from the chalice of grief,
and its acid corrodes me within.

Tongueless to mouth
this devastation,
my heart is harrowed
in a desert of despair,

and swallowed in sinking sands
of sorrow,
I thirst for the oasis
that was you.

XVIII

Take me back
down the vista of years
to where a tropical sun
burns its way
through the fabric of island sky.

Take me back
to that country village
where the cane fields rise
in the winnowing wind
and hummingbirds vie
to kiss hibiscus flowers.

She is there
in that old, wooden house,
with its galvanized roof
and shuttered windows,
where resurrected memories
haunt my dreams;

she is there
on the front porch,
smiling.

XIX

I think of Lucy
mother to us all,
Australopithecus afarensis
who carried the yoke
of all humanity
within her primitive shell,

that how, after millennia
and succeeding generations
her DNA yet strands us
to our common past.

So am I stranded to you
and you, to me
both of us, a reflection
of the other.

XX

So much was lost
the day you went away,
each of our hearts
imploding into pieces
each piece,
a part of you.

We wear the scars
of each chip and crack
that only the light of love reveals,
exposing the whole of our
            bro-
                    keness.

All that remains is a shattering,
a scattering of us
that was you.

The Radha Poems

XXI

Six o'clock
evening sky burns
the horizon's rim
as day dissolves into night.

In this hour of vespers
I call to you,
and you are there
in the candle's flickering flame,
your luminescent aura
enveloping me
with the light of your
tender love.

I tell you how my day was
cutting open my heart
till the blood of life spills
from confessing lips,

but you say nothing,
nothing at all,
you just listen to my ramblings
knowing full well
all I'll ever need
is to feel you by my side.

XXII

No,
you will not convince me
she is gone,
that the essence of her being
is lost.

You have taken the body
but not the spirit,
for that which is her
will always exist,
though eyes cannot see her
nor hands ever touch her
nor ears ever hear
the melody of her voice,

she still lives in the heart
that forever loves,
she still lives in the mind
that believes.

XXIII

I'm having trouble
referring to you
in the past tense.

She was...
you were...

Sometimes,
the heart refuses
to truly acknowledge
what the brain shapes into language.

Sometimes,
the brain is incapable
of fully grasping
what the heart cannot let go of.

XXIV

Do not be afraid
though Death has taken you
by your silent heart
and led you away
from here.

Do not be sad
for this lease on life expired,
for the people and places
you leave behind,

for I am always with you
and you, with me
two souls connected
in spirit and flesh
across space and time,
life and death,
by the umbilical cord
of Love.

XXV

Give the body back to the earth,
every bone, every tooth
every atom that was loaned
to dress the spirit with matter.

Give them all back
to the fire that feeds
upon the frailty of flesh
in a final consummation of clay.

Release the essence
of all we were,
gleaned from the experience
of this human condition
back into the beauty
of the universal void,

into that which forever remains.

XXVI

No,
do not go yet,
do not leave me alone
to greet the light of day.

Stay a little while longer,
let me gaze upon the face
I've loved all my life
and hear the sweet cadence
of your tender voice;
let me bask in the warmth
of your luminous smile
if only for a minute more.

Nothing awaits me
in the world of the living,
save the pain of knowing
you no longer share
the same reality as I.

Let me not yet be
the ghost I will become,
awakened to be haunted
by resurrected memories.

The Radha Poems

In dreams, I am alive
with you who cannot die
you, whose very presence
infuses my heart with joy,

so stay, stay with me
a little while longer,
for it is not the robin
that will sing me awake,

it is you,
beloved you.

XXVII

Take the essence of spirit
and flesh it with earth
till it becomes confined
in this human shell,
believing what it filters
through its sieve of senses;

but strip the spirit
of its mortal garb,
and it becomes exposed
to a beautiful truth:

the universality of Love.

The Radha Poems

XXVIII

The beauty of this world has faded
for you are no longer here,
now my hollowed heart is jaded
by an all-consuming fear.

A sadness has awakened within me
a sadness that never dies,
for all I loved so dearly
was lost when you closed your eyes.

XXIX

Blue Child,
why do you cry so much?
Do you long to see her sweet face?
Do you miss her tender touch?

Your life has been in shambles
and full of so much pain,
since she has gone away
and will not come again.

Blue Child, do not grieve so
for there within your heart,
she will live forever
and nevermore shall part.

XXX

I've come to realize,
in the vast continuum
of space and time,
life and death are the same;
each a reflection of the other
in the perpetual becoming
and evolution
of the unborn soul.

The Radha Poems

XXXI

This is the first Spring without you,
the first chirping of the robin
you will not hear,
the first blooming of the rose, unseen.

In this season of renewal
when life resurrects
from the dormancy of winter dreams,
that which is missed
always comes back
to comfort the heart in need.

But you are not here
though the trees are awakening
to the wind's wild rapture
of song,

you are not here
though the bees are pollinating
the flowers in their
blossoming throng.

Whatever wonders the season bears
however bright its hue,
there is no beauty within the world,
no Springtime, without you.

XXXII

My heart is a black hole
without you,
the collapsed remains
of an imploded star.

Whatever joy I had,
whatever peace of mind,
can never escape
grief's gravity.

XXXIII

Take me on a tachyon trip
backwards in time
to when the summer wind strummed
the trees like harps
on a blue and breezy afternoon.

Let me relive
that moment in memory
at the picnic tables
in Wishing Well Park
when we sat together
and ate cheese sandwiches
beneath the maple's embroidery of leaves.

Take me back to Frisbees
slicing through the sky,
and the sound of your laughter
among green grassed fields,
let me linger here awhile
to remember what it was like
to taste the sweet flavour of joy;
here with the shadows
of my long-lost past
and you ... beautiful you.

XXXIV

What does it matter to the world
that one candle should burn out
among 8 billion?
Or that one flame should be
extinguished
in a firmament of stars?

It matters to me

for the day you died
the lights went out in each of us,
a chain reaction
of burnt-out hearts
in a grid over-gloomed
by grief.

XXXV

Loss,
a small word
of such magnitude.

Ask the heart
how difficult it is
to carry its weight
and it will answer in agony:

unbearable .

XXXVI

Grief crushes my lungs
till I gasp for air,
knowing that your body
does not breathe anymore.

XXXVII

The first flowers of Spring
have sprung,
as trees awaken
to the wind's caress
in this season of Beauty's rebirth,

and yet,
my heart can find no solace
in the chorus of the cardinal's song,
can take no pleasure
in the loveliness of leaves
when ah,
Sweet Soul,
Bird of Paradise,

you were everything beautiful
        to me.

XXXVIII

Suena de los angelitos

I remember you singing
in the living years,
your voice as sweet
as any angel's,
as beautiful as any bird's.

Now you sing to me in dreams,
your spirit shining
in a symphony of souls
serenading me awake
from afar.

XXXIX

*Grief is the ashes
love bequeaths to our hearts.*

How to articulate this pain
that penetrates to the core
of my being?

How to verbalize a loss
so profound,
it alters me from within

into something,
someone,
unrecognizable without?

XL

I still see you at the stove
in your kitchen,
sunlight tangled in your auburn hair
the smell of your cooking
engulfing the house
in a sweet, aromatic wave.

Whatever meals you prepared
however grand or small
you seasoned with the flavour
    of love,
a taste my tongue
will always remember
and my heart
will forever crave.

XLI

The truth is
I didn't deserve you,
none of us did.

That I should be the beneficiary
of your unconditional love,
of a blessing so precious
to the heart and soul

can never be justified
nor ever accepted
without feelings of
unworthiness and guilt.

The Radha Poems

XLII

Your face was the first
      I ever saw,
angelic oval, shining bright
with sequin stars in your eyes.

Your voice was the first
      I ever heard,
sweet warbler, serenading me
to sleep with your song.

Now your beauty has gone away
and lost in this dreary world,
I look for the light
that is your love
to lead me back to you
someday.

XLIII

Radiant/red plumed/songbird
Ascended/absolved/of flesh and fear
Devoted/mother/matriarch
Hero/hoisted/heavenwards
Angel/of my heart/hereafter.

XLIV

I have been intimate with Grief
    this past year,
called her sweet names
in the hollow of night
when my tight chest heaves
beneath the weight of fears.

She whispers pure heartache
    into my ear,
brushes my hair back
and collects my tears
in the merciless palms
    of her hands.

Before she leaves
I taste her kiss,
bitter upon my trembling lips
and sink into a dreamless void
while she sings me to sleep
again and again
with her lullabies of loss
and longing.

XLV

In the schoolyard,
flag at half mast,
teachers and parents come together
in a circle of love
around your little tree.

After the speeches and photographs
when tears were shed and
hearts beat heavy,
one by one
they paid their respects
with snow white flowers
beside your plaque
in honour of Miss Radha's memory.

At ceremony's end
the crowds dispersed
as children brought you gifts
of dandelions,

their voices of gratitude
carried by the wind
into a sombre April sky.

XLVI

Eight months now
and I still mourn you,
my wounds raw
and open to grief's infection.

Not that grief has a time limit
or expiration date;
it doesn't.

It just comes and goes
like a rising tide,
advancing and receding
to and fro,
independent of the moon's gravity.

For now,
the best I can do
is plug the holes
in my boat of resilience,
take a deep breath
and hope to survive
its next tsunami.

XLVII

Mother's Day,
and I'm reminded of the blessing
that was you.

In the lifeless living room
next to your picture
I place purple flowers
in a crystal vase,
reminiscent of the blossoms
I picked for you as a child.

In time
like all things material,
they too will wither and fade
till all that remains
is the memory of their beauty;

much like what you have bequeathed
to each of us,
when after ashes to ashes
and dust to dust,
the memory of your kindness,
your gentleness, your love

makes you forever beautiful
        to me.

XLVIII

I look up at the night sky
replete with grains of stars,
a whirling wonder
of light and dark
scattered across galaxies of time;

think of the physicists
and their far-out theories,
like the quantum possibility
of an infinite multiverse;
try to wrap my mind
around the magnitude of matter
and the probable implications.

I don't know if they're right
or just stringing us along,
but the thought of living
parallel lives
in alternate realities
across different dimensions,
brings me comfort
knowing there's a chance
that somewhere out there
beyond my dreams
in a universe far, far away,
you're still alive and beautiful
and forever, that way, will stay.

XLIX

Inconsolable heart,
there is no needle or thread
that can bind together
the gaping hole of your grief;
no staple or suture
strong enough
to stop you from your heavy bleeding.

Unglued by her death
you crack and crumble,
till all that remains
of your former self
is the memory of her love
for you.

L

Who will remember me when I am gone?
When my soul no longer
inhabits this flesh?

In whose memories will I still live on?
What vigils will be kept
for me?

Time afflicts the living with amnesia
and our presence, erases away
till all that remains
are shadows of our past,
the sad obituaries of our yesterdays.

But you, dear Mother
shall not suffer such a fate,
for destined are the blessed
to be

resurrected by our love
to live forever
in the heart and in memory.

LI

This is my first birthday
without you,
and all I can feel
is an emptiness of being
when your absence clings to my heart.

Amid the candle lit cake
and celebration
believing in wishes come true,
I close my eyes
and long to hear
you sing, *Happy Birthday, to You.*

LII

Your death changed my life;
forced me to face
my own mortality
in a world full of shadows
and strange illusions
that confound and deceive the mind.

You no longer *are*
and yet, you *are*
just as I am not
but forever will be
on planes of existence
beyond our own,
in alternate realities.

Then what is death
if not an awakening
to that which we cannot see?

My belief will birth
that sweet hereafter
and immortalize both you
and me.

LIII

What is death
if not the body's surrendering
to life?

The experience is ephemeral;
a temporary visa
allowing us to travel
through space and time
where, at journey's end
when the flesh expires

we give back to the earth,
to the universal void,
each singular atom
that was loaned to us,
and doff the corporeal
to once again
reawaken
to our spiritual selves.

The Radha Poems

LIV

Sometimes I feel like
you're still here,
that at any given moment
you'll surely reappear.

Tomorrow, I'll grow older
with every passing day,
till the face I wear upon me
will crack and fade away.

But will you recognize me
when my living years are done?
Will you still remember
the visage of your son?

    Ask me who I am
and I'll answer so you'll know,

*I was the boy who picked you flowers
a long, long time ago.*

LV

Somewhere,
stitched into my memory,
is a thread that binds me
to my distant past.

Arc of wing wind-whirled
in a blue dome of sky,

shriek of gull
pulling me back
to my childhood years,
like the water's undertow
off a sandy beach,

the weightlessness of body
being swept away
and you, a lifeguard of love,
your liquid voice
rising on the waves.
the comfort of your arms
around me...

Endless summer
tropical sun,
a stitch in memory
comes undone.

LVI

You were the center of everything,
a force of gravity
around which our hearts
revolved in elliptic rings.

Now, you have vanished
and tossed out of orbit,
we haunt the galaxy
in search of grace,
nomads in the nothingness
of space and time,

fading to oblivion
without a trace.

LVII

What is the circumference of grief
that it should encompass
the breadth of our being?

How to identify its edges
and define its parameters
when it constantly morphs
into something new,
into a shape without any structure?

Bleed a heart full of grief
with the memory of love,
and watch it splatter

into infinite fractals.

The Radha Poems

LVIII

Give me this moment
to celebrate you.

You were my hero,
the champion of my childhood years
and conqueror of
all fears.

You were the light
that enlightened my gloom,
a nurse to the needs of my troubled mind
when trapped in a mental cocoon.

And though you shunned the spotlight
and shied away from view,
oh, to possess such a heart as yours,
oh, to be just like you.

The Radha Poems

LIX

Let me paint your portrait
with words.

Shy smile
as gentle as a summer breeze,
fine lips and jaw,
a porcelain chin,
warm oval face
upon whose cheeks
a garden of roses yet bloom.

Wisp of winter fire
in your auburn hair,
bright eyes, as tender
as an autumn dawn,
small nose, lobed ears
a refined brow,
untouched and untarnished
by the talons of time.

A beautiful masterpiece
shall you always be,
for all with eyes
to read and see.

LX

We've walked together
on this winding road
for so many years,
seen the seasons come and go
through earth's diurnal course,
felt the stinging rain upon our faces
and the warmth of forgiving suns.

In the early days, you held my hand
when time was young and life seemed
an awakening to a beautiful dream,
till I learned to run ahead of you
eager to explore the world.

Over the hills and through the valleys
you were my true companion,
a source of strength
from which my heart
quenched its thirst for love.

The Radha Poems

When your steps grew weary
in those final days,
I held your hand
at chapter's end,
where the road forked out
to signal the start
of your story's new beginning.

For where the spirit goes
flesh cannot follow,
and so, we brave the journey alone,
knowing in our hearts
that along the way,
our paths will converge someday.

The Radha Poems

LXI

On a bookshelf in the basement
your picture books rest,
the archival remnants
of your grandmother dreams.

Beneath the collected dust
of accumulated years
they remain unopened,
frozen in time,
never to be shared
with a longed-for grandchild,
never to be read
out of love.

LXII

Caught in the fray and fury of it all,
I'm wind-whipped in a whirling whiteout
where my eyes cannot see you
nor my hands feel your touch.

Tossed and turned and torn within,
I fearfully freefall into the unknown
not yet a spirit freed from flesh
but in a discombobulation of being.

This sonorous storm scowls and screams
and delights in devouring
my desires and dreams.
It swallows me whole and hurls me about,
till I wander weathered,
withered, and without.

LXIII

Time is a river of memories
flowing through my veins,
pulling me deeper into myself,
its current – a cord
that tethers me to your love.

Whatever strength I have left
        to carry on,
to keep swimming against
   grief's grasping waves,
  I inherited from you,
     bright angelfish,

none as valiant as you.

LXIV

I found an old photo
of you and me,
a little window offering
a momentary glimpse
into the lives we left behind.

You are young and beautiful
with a river of hair
flowing and fragrant,
as in my dreams,
holding me close
in your loving arms
from some long-ago time, it seems.

Sweet Angel,
who carried me all those years
even when your bones
grew weary with time,

I will carry you now
    within me,
and make of your memory
    a beacon,
to guide me down
life's path of thorns
till I find my way back to you.

The Radha Poems

LXV

    Rest now
for your work here is done.

The cups and dishes
have been cleared from the table,
the floor is swept
and the sun hangs low
in the evening sky.

Good Mother,
your children are grown
and have fluttered far
from your empty nest,

no more bruises to kiss
or lullabies to sing,
no more broken hearts
in need of mending.

Come lay your head down
on a pillow of dreams
and close your eyes
in eternal sleep,
be at peace with the life
you leave behind,

Good Mother,
 be at peace.

LXVI

From birth to death, the cycle is complete
for the soul now takes that final climb
to where flesh cannot spirit meet,
but must remain in space and time.

The life we all leave behind us
is one of illusion and dream,
we suffer this human experience
for the spirit in us to redeem.

Blessed is she who receives
God's gift of love to keep.

*Good Mother, you are awakened
it is I who am still asleep.*

LXVII

You are everywhere
and in everything now.

All that you were,
are, and yet will be
is manifested in the microcosm
    of this reality,
mirrored in all aspects
of what we deem to be.

I'll see you in every flower
hear your voice in birdsong,
feel your gentle touch
in every drop of rain;
whatever beauty you possessed
will be reflected in nature
to inform my senses
that you are here with me.

Then why should I grieve
for having lost that
which was never taken away from me?

I will brave the wild wind
and breathe you in,
till my spirit shimmers with your beauty.

LXVIII

You will always be beautiful to me.

Come, let us walk together
for the hours grow shorter
and the evening sky
is burning away at its edges.

Autumn hangs on the horizon now,
a strawberry cluster of clouds
that ripens with each passing day.

Soon, the trees will blush
blood orange,
and ribbons of birds
will brave the skies
in search of perpetual summers,

while as yet, the dandelions
still cry out,
their yellow voices
fading in the wind
to a distant ... *remember us.*

The Radha Poems

I know you too, must go
must say goodbye and
leave behind
all the things that you love so.

Fear not the road that lies ahead
nor that journey into the unknown,
for wherever you are
and whatever you do
   Good Mother,

my love will find you.

The Radha Poems

GLOSSARY

Australopithecus afarensis: An extinct, early human species of australopithecine which lived from about 3.9 to about 2.9 million years ago.

Bhajan: Devotional song with a religious theme or spiritual idea.

Suena de los angelitos: Spanish for 'dream with the angels'.

Twameva mata cha pita twameva: Traditional Hindu prayer.

The Radha Poems

Author Profile

Jeevan Bhagwat lives in Scarborough, Ontario. His work has been widely published in literary journals/websites such as The Queen's Quarterly, Windsor Review, Poetry Pause, The Prairie Journal, and his work will be forthcoming in Canadian Literature. In 2003 and 2005, he won The Monica Ladell Prize for Poetry from the Scarborough Arts Council and in 2015 he was the recipient of the Scarborough Urban Hero Award for Arts & Culture. He is the co-facilitator of the Scarborough Poetry Club. His poetry books include The Weight of Dreams (IN Publications, 2012) and Luminescence (IN Publications, 2020)

www.ingramcontent.com/pod-product-compliance
Lightning Source LLC
Chambersburg PA
CBHW052150070526
44585CB00017B/2061